—— CONTE

CHOICE

Juana Adcock • *Split* • Blue Diode Press

RECOMMENDATIONS

Charlotte Ansell • *Deluge* • flipped eye
Kwame Dawes & John Kinsella • *Tangling with the Epic* • Peepal Tree Press
Denise Riley • *Selected Poems* • Picador
Zoë Skoulding • *Footnotes to Water* • Seren

SPECIAL COMMENDATION

Charlotte Mew • *Selected Poetry and Prose* • Edited by Julia Copus • Faber

RECOMMENDED TRANSLATION

Esther Dischereit • *Sometimes a Single Leaf* • Arc Publications
Translated by Iain Galbraith

PAMPHLET CHOICE

Amy Acre • *And They Are Covered in Gold Light* • Bad Betty Press

WILD CARD

Mimi Khalvati • *Afterwardness* • Carcanet Press

REVIEWS
LISTINGS

Poetry Book Society

CHOICE SELECTORS RECOMMENDATION SPECIAL COMMENDATION	SANDEEP PARMAR & VIDYAN RAVINTHIRAN
TRANSLATION SELECTOR	GEORGE SZIRTES
PAMPHLET SELECTORS	A.B. JACKSON & DEGNA STONE
WILD CARD SELECTOR	ANTHONY ANAXAGOROU
CONTRIBUTORS	SOPHIE O'NEILL NATHANIEL SPAIN
GUEST REVIEWER	JADE CUTTLE
EDITORIAL & DESIGN	ALICE KATE MULLEN

Membership Options

Magazine (Associate) 4 *Bulletins* a year (UK £22, Europe £35, Rest of the World £42)

Choice (Full) 4 Choice books and 4 *Bulletins* a year (£55, £65, £75)

Charter 20 books and 4 *Bulletins* (£180, £210, £235)

School Basic 4 books, 4 *Bulletins*, posters, teaching notes (£79, £89, £99)

School Advanced 20 books, 4 *Bulletins*, posters, teaching notes (£209, £245, £275)

Translation 4 Translation books and 4 *Bulletins* (£65, £90, £99)

Student 4 Choice books and 4 *Bulletins* (£35, £55, £65)

Translation Plus Full 4 Choices, 4 *Bulletins* & 4 Translation books (£98, £120, £132)

Complete 20 books, 4 *Bulletins* & 4 Translation books (£223, £265, £292)

Single copies of the *Bulletin* £9.99

Cover Art Angela T. Carr **Website** www.adreamingskin.com

Copyright Poetry Book Society and contributors. All rights reserved.
ISBN 9781913129101 ISSN 0551-1690

Poetry Book Society | Milburn House | Dean Street | Newcastle upon Tyne | NE1 1LF
0191 230 8100 | enquiries@poetrybooksociety.co.uk

WWW.POETRYBOOKS.CO.UK

LETTER FROM THE PBS

This season's *Bulletin* embodies much of what we have tried to achieve over the last three years of running the PBS – striving to present to you the best of contemporary poetry, with insightful reviews and commentary. Behind the scenes, much effort has gone into ensuring the PBS welcomes all poetry publishers to submit work to our PBS selectors. So we are delighted this season's Choice, Juana Adcock is a lesser known poet published by a brand new publishing company Blue Diode Press. Here's hoping the same critical success follows on from her PBS selection as with many of our other Choices.

It's a diverse selection this winter, collections from new poets, established poets, neglected poets, we have them all! As ever, we love to hear your thoughts, both positive and constructive, so please do let us know what you think of the selections, your membership, or anything else poetry-related either through our social media channels, over email or phone – we genuinely love to hear from you.

Thanks to everyone who came to our National Poetry Day celebrations at the wonderful Blackwell's in Oxford; Mary Jean Chan and Anthony Anaxagorou gave stunning performances. Our next event is a Translation Conference, taking place in Norwich on 30th November, tickets are available through our website, so please do come along.

Christmas is not so far away, so do consider giving the gift of poetry this Christmas – you can buy PBS gift memberships or simply a PBS gift-voucher and let the recipient choose to go wild on book purchases or a membership. Keep an eye on our website www.poetrybooks.co.uk and across social media @poetrybooksoc for more poetic gift inspiration throughout the festive season.

SOPHIE O'NEILL
PBS & INPRESS DIRECTOR

JUANA ADCOCK

Juana Adcock is a poet, translator and performer working in English and Spanish. Her poems and translations have been published in magazines such as *Magma*, *Structo*, *Words without Borders*, *Asymptote*, *Kenyon Review*, *Gutter*, *Glasgow Review of Books*, *New Writing Scotland*, *The Dark Horse* and several anthologies in Mexico and the UK. Her first collection, *Manca* (Tierra Adentro, 2014) explored the anatomy of violence in Mexico. In 2016, Adcock was named one of the Top Ten New Voices From Europe by Literary Europe Live and Literature Across Frontiers, and she has performed at numerous festivals internationally. In 2006 she received a year-long writing fellowship from CONARTE in Mexico, and in 2016 she was awarded a Scottish artists' fellowship to complete a writing residency in Banff, Canada. She has lived in Glasgow since 2007, where she also plays in the bands Las Mitras and The Raptors.

CHOICE

SPLIT

BLUE DIODE PRESS | £10.00 | PBS PRICE   £7.50

Juana Adcock's second collection, *Split*, opens with a long sequence of 'Serpent Dialogues' between a woman and a snake. Part Genesis, part Plato, the two debate "the true nature of desire", among other things.

WOMAN: Snake, what do you think of monotheism? Since everything is holy, I mean
SNAKE: Men – humans – need to organize everything. Messages need to be packaged in a way that's intelligible to them, otherwise they'd be lost.
W: That's why the Mass is didactic in structure, like a theatre play, is what you're saying
S: Yes, but the sacred element is also built through repetition. Repetition is much loved by men
W: You don't dislike it either, since you come here to see me every day
S: It's nice on this rock
W: There are countless others to choose from

The combination of seduction, lovers' anxiety, mortal danger and philosophy works extremely well, dosed up by a mix of irony and vulnerability that is delivered so directly it is occasionally devastating. Reminiscent of Anne Carson's dialogic poetic work, Adcock's formal dexterity throughout this collection testifies to the breadth of her intellectual enquiry and her literary inheritance. Adcock's first collection was published in 2014 in Mexico, where she was born (she now lives in Scotland). Mexico appears in this book, too, via ancient mythical as well as contemporary political references, as in the poem 'Juárez / Ecatepec': "I was looking, in vain, for the newspaper article / that told our story among the deluge of pages // on the thousands of women of similar fates." Most readers should be aware of the decades-long murder, rape and disappearances of female factory workers in the border city of Juárez, Mexico. These crimes implicate male violence at every level of authority and yet the killings have not ended. Adcock's poem is brutally honest – she presents the ubiquity of these deaths through the eyes of the murdered as well as those who are unable to prevent their continuation.

Other poems here are similarly engaged in the politics of language, race, gender, all the while making dazzling manoeuvres that challenge the dominance of inward-looking lyricism in our times of wider collective consciousness. *Split* is a hugely original and vital book, one I did not see coming, that raises the stakes for contemporary British poetry.

SANDEEP PARMAR

JUANA ADCOCK

My book *Split* owes a great deal to a ground-breaking book by the Mexican poet Óscar David López, titled *Perro semihundido*, or *Half-Sunken Dog*, which I translated into English and am hoping to publish. A long poem written from the point of view of a stray dog, it uses footnotes to subvert the boundaries between marginal and mainstream, waste and product, dog and master.

For Donna Haraway, the dog's gaze is the gaze of the absolute other, as the dog has no language, yet exists in relation to us. She wrote that "dog writing should be a branch of feminist theory, or the other way around." Eileen Myles said at a reading in Glasgow from her book *Afterglow* (*A Dog Memoir*) that "dog narratives are queer narratives," and Hélène Cixous went further, saying that whoever is incapable of listening to the dog's voice, will be incapable of listening to that "of a woman or a Jew or an Arab or any subject belonging to one of these species which carry the fate of banishment." It seemed to me that López's entire poem was an act of translation, in its attempt to articulate the language of this absolute other. The idea of a dialogue between humans and animals has captured my imagination since then.

After a real-life encounter with a snake during a solitary writing retreat in Italy, which was also a head-on encounter with my own fears/desires, I thought about actually listening to what the snake had to say. The figure of the snake was interesting to me as it is not traditionally thought of as a companion species but rather as a symbol of humanity's sin and banishment, and thus even less worthy of being heard. This was the framework within which I also started listening to the parts of myself which I was afraid to acknowledge, and how they might relate to the "fear of the other" which is currently so present in the world.

JUANA RECOMMENDS

Rebecca Tamás, *WITCH* (Penned in the Margins); Lisa Fannen, *Faultline* (Active Distribution); Joshua Whitehead, *full-metal indigiqueer* (Talonbooks); Inger Christensen, *it*, translated by Susanna Nied (Carcanet Press); Marosa di Giorgio, *I Remember Nightfall*, translated by Jeannine Marie Pitas (Ugly Duckling Presse), Antoine Cassar, *Bejn / Between* (Skarta); Janet Paisley, *Sang fur the Wandert* (Luath Press) and Sasha Pimentel, *For Want of Water* (Beacon Press).

I CHOICE

SKIRT OF SNAKES

In the anthropology museum
in Mexico City

the statue
of Coatlicue

wears a skirt of woven snakes
a necklace of human hearts and hands

her breasts heavy from gravidanza
the clasp of her belt a skull.

And where she was decapitated
her spurting blood is two facing serpents.

Voracious monster mother
loving Earth mother

   tomb /
womb, etc.

She rises at dawn to sweep away the bones
make space for the new

her son
fathered by a feather

is born
fully grown

armoured
for battle.

We, his snake sisters
weave

THE POET ATTEMPTS TO BUILD A HOUSE (EXTRACT)

Carve one brick
to perfection
my word my word

embers at the pit
of my belly

I blow slow smoke
to cool off
the spill
hardening to rock

I carve and
cart the words to
my plot

my legs like a compass
measure out the land

where I must flatten grassblades
dig out pits

an economy of guilt

CHARLOTTE ANSELL

Charlotte Ansell is the author of *you were for the poem* and *After Rain*. A dedicated boat-dweller, her poems have appeared in *Poetry Review, Mslexia, Now Then, Butcher's Dog, Prole, Algebra of Owls* and various anthologies. She won the Red Shed Open Poetry Competition and was one of six finalists in the BBC Write Science competition in 2015. Charlotte recently left Yorkshire via the North Sea to moor up on the Medway and *Deluge*, her third poetry collection, partly reflects her close relationship to water.

DELUGE

FLIPPED   EYE | £6.95 | PBS   PRICE   £5.22

A POETRY BOOK SOCIETY RECOMMENDATION

CHARLOTTE ANSELL
DELUGE

Has Brexit torn England in two? We've the feeling of splitting into tribes. For one thing, there's London, and "the North":

> We bring our London ways north
> suspicious of the stranger on the towpath
> who asks: *Are we settling in alright?*
> my head in a book on the train,
> not joining in the chat
> thinking; surely these women
> can't have just met?
> -'Flat Caps And Ferrets'

The poems cherish rootedness – "This knife is Sheffield born / out of the streams, stones / and tors of the Peaks" – but also speak of moving from where you're comfortable (or familiarly uneasy) to what may as well be, and sometimes actually is, a foreign land. "Lacerate all ties", this poem ends, "as you walk away from the town / that was never yours." In 'Where they burn books...' the speaker doubts herself at a school play: "I'm grateful when Sky's mum sits next to me / until she complains that Sky, / with a tea towel round her head / is being turned into a paki." The poet chooses words carefully: the name 'Sky', even, and the malignity of "being turned into", which spotlights a racist undertone as well as an overtone.

Place names evince a plainspoken matter-of-factness which doesn't, however, rule out deftness: "the subdued pale of a Tottenham / morning"; 'Welcome to Scarborough YHA' (a title, one of several, conjuring a precise locale):

> Aspirations get lost between Steel St and Holmes Lock
> as generations draw dole cheques,
> forget what it is to bring home a wage;
>
> - 'This is Why We Can't Have Nice Things'
>
> We were going places though, weren't we?
> All the must-see destinations;
> Helsinki, Pescara, Hull.
>
> -'Not Ever After'

This is the brave opposite of navel-gazing – the poetry of Charlotte Ansell keeps a close eye on the world.

VIDYAN RAVINTHIRAN

SELECTOR'S COMMENT

CHARLOTTE ANSELL

The word "deluge" has its roots in the Latin "diluvium". *The Chambers 21st Century Dictionary* defines it as 1. a flood. 2. a downpour of rain. 3. a great quantity of anything coming or pouring in. Verb – to be deluged by something – to be overwhelmed by it. This is how life can feel sometimes, how I have felt in these poems; sometimes literally, sometimes figuratively.

Roger Deakin observed that we have webbing between our thumbs and forefingers, supporting the notion that we are drawn to water biologically as well as philosophically. In *How to Read Water*, Tristan Gooley quotes the anthropologist Loren Eiseley: "If there is magic on this planet, it is contained in water". Which naturally leads me to Larkin's conjuring of water as religion in his eminent Water poem. For me, it is not so much a religion I have constructed, as a life; as a boat dweller, wild swimmer and pluviophile.

Water is never far away then; these are poems drenched by rain or cradled by rivers, canals, lakes and the sea, all of these aspects being potentially treacherous and life sustaining in equal measure. This is why these are also very often poems of struggle, mine and others, perhaps best summarised in these lines from my final poem, 'Containment':

> Who doesn't need to feel held,
> contained by a vessel
> without holes, however small;
> no one needs the kind of life
> that leaks like a sieve...

Gooley also asserts that water is attracted to itself; it has a stickiness powerful enough to resist gravity's pull. When spilt, water will form droplets drawn to each other. Water may more traditionally be thought of as a carrier and here I hope it is all these things; it is what draws the poems together and holds them.

CHARLOTTE RECOMMENDS

Clare Shaw, *Flood* (Bloodaxe Books); Raymond Antrobus, *The Perserverance* (Penned in the Margins); Liz Berry, *Black Country* (Chatto & Windus); Fran Lock, *Dogtooth* (Outspoken Press); Ian Humphreys, *Zebra* (Nine Arches Press); Kim Moore, *The Art of Falling* (Seren); Joelle Taylor, *Songs my enemy taught me* (Outspoken Press) and because books are expensive, these poems online: 'Why I left you' by Selima Hill, www.poetryarchive.org; 'How to date a white boy' by Amy Alvarez, www.rattle.com, and 'Roadkill' by T'ai Freedom Ford, www.poems.com.

RECOMMENDATION

It isn't the big things that capsize us

Image: Zigmunds Lapsa

DELUGE

The sky
is a steel sheet
riveted over the door
of a repossessed flat.
Our car on the way home
is battered, as gusts threaten to
swerve us into the outside lane, rain
hits the windscreen leaving marks like
cigarette burns before they dissipate. We are
cocooned, blinded, stunned by the force; but we've
survived worse. Like last summer, when the canal's level rose
ever closer to the lock gates, all twelve foot of them, putting our trust
in ballast and ropes, the three in the morning checks. I didn't anticipate I'd spend
my life fighting or that abundance could be this depriving as the rain continued
to fall and fall, only ever down. At primary school my teacher called me stoic
(she meant stubborn) I was the kind of child who refused to go out to play;
if she made me, I took my book to a bench. Five years in the north
we have been deluged, swamped; by bills, demands,
increasing costs, as the water outside oblivious
to us creeps higher, finds the gaps. Cheap boots
didn't last the winter, the damp seeps into my
toes, the hatches leak onto the beds.
In this decade, it's not about us
anymore, a flood would take
the children too if we let it.
If we didn't keep bailing out,
scraping by, paying
with hours,
tired eyes,
prayers.

KWAME DAWES

JOHN KINSELLA

Kwame Dawes is the author of over thirty-five books, and is widely recognized as one of the Caribbean's leading writers. Elected as a Chancellor of the Academy of American Poets, Dawes is also an honorary FRSL. He is the co-founder and programming director of the Calabash International Literary Festival in Jamaica. He is the Glenna Luschei Editor of *Prairie Schooner* at the University of Nebraska, where he is a Chancellor's Professor of English. Dawes is the founding director of the African Poetry Book Fund and teaches in the Pacific MFA Program in Oregon.

John Kinsella's books of poetry include *Armour* (Picador, 2010), *Jam Tree Gully* (W.W. Norton, 2012) and *Drowning in Wheat: Selected Poems* (Picador, 2016). He is a Fellow of Churchill College, Cambridge University, and Professor of Literature and Sustainability at Curtin University. Kinsella has received many awards, including the Australian Prime Minister's Award for Poetry and the John Bray Award for Poetry from the Adelaide Festival.

TANGLING WITH THE EPIC

PEEPAL TREE | £10.99 | PBS PRICE £8.25

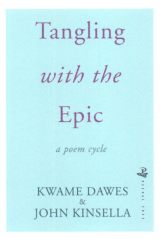

Tangling with the Epic is John Kinsella and Kwame Dawes' third in a quartet of book-length poem-dialogues. The book is comprised of alternating initialled nine-line poems in Spenserian stanzas, each man writing from their distinct geographical and racial positioning to discuss a range of subjects including – unsurprisingly, given the poets' individual oeuvres – political and ecological turmoil. As a vehicle for the building of nation-myths, the epic reigns supreme across the globe and its ancient formal variations (and modern equivalents), make it worthy of critique and, perhaps in this case, inhabitation. Spenser's *Faerie Queene* this is not, but what we have here in place of allegory and chivalry is a sense of the pastoral and moral authority of man and nature. Trump looms large, colonialism, too. This conversation is a working out of national mythologies – it is tangling with, as much as it is untangling, the epic proportions of Australian and American nativism. Sometimes this happens with directness, elsewhere the pastoral speaks encoded within the mind of the observer who knows the landscape intimately.

> The truth is, John, lately I've been tracing
> the curious history of this republic,
> sure that deep in its DNA is lurking
> a carefully buried clue, a relic
> that just might explain the reign of this sick
> despot. All I have found is human folly,
> the canker of old hubris, the politics
> eating away at our bodies each day;
> then carnage, then death, then just maybe, brand new days!

Kinsella replies to Dawes, bringing the intimacy of illness, to the body politic.

> Things aren't quite right for me post-accident.
> Something lost, and what has been gained is that
> form of second sight that doesn't give vent,
> doesn't operate as a thermostat.
> Something rotten in the Republic's heart
> speaks to what's rotten in the Commonwealth,
> underwritten by the theft of land, straight
> from the ancient to the modern, such stealth-
> technology the military calls our health.

With the fast-pace of political, ecological and social change, one can't help but wonder what the next few years, and this dialogue's last volume, have in store for us.

18 SANDEEP PARMAR

JOHN KINSELLA

Kwame and I have been working together on writing dialogue-poems for quite a few years now. This is the third volume in a cycle of four, in which we tell our separate life-journeys so often finding common ground in the expression of our different experiences, geographies, ancestries, and embodiments. It is an act of mutual respect.

We had been largely using open form poems in our earlier volumes, and decided we wanted to push our conversation further by working with constraint – we decided on the Spenserian stanza as technically challenging but also highly fluid and lending itself to accumulation and "story-telling." It's an easy stanza to get into the rhythm of, and is a good vehicle for narrative, but it also comes with a disturbing colonising irony and in our efforts to consider our lives in the context of the machinations of a conflicted world, we were inevitably going to push up against the walls of this form, and its origins and subsequent histories. We wished to make, through undoing, the history of the form itself.

Kwame and I wanted to make and unmake an epic poem in the same breath (or breaths), to journey through both shared and private space/s, and to reconcile, if possible, inner and outer worlds. The poem is a documenting of where the observer sits in relation to cascading injustice and damage in the world at large, but with frequent interludes of wonder and contact with people, the natural world, and "the word". This is an anti-colonial anti-epic that tries to find belief in living and affirmation in community, against the odds. Each poem is an utterance against greed and indifference to life, and in such, I hope, instead of particular heroes arising, a collective indomitability of the "human" is spoken. It's not a poem of nations or greatness, but a poem of people resisting harm, and of us finding a way of talking under all conditions of stress.

JOHN RECOMMENDS

The Collected Poems of Edouard Glissant, translated by Jeff Humphries (University of Minnesota Press, 2005); *Nganajungu Yagu* by Charmaine Papertalk-Green (Cordite Books, 2019); and a return (yet again) to *Peacock Blue: The Collected Poems of Phyllis Webb*, edited by John F. Hulcoop (Talonbooks, 2014).

KWAME DAWES

What I say here, about this collaboration, is going to be inadequate and limited in its usefulness in assessing the relative value of the work John Kinsella and I have produced. What I can say is that I have been pleased, moved and proud of the poems we have been exchanging, of the way that we challenge each other, not so much with notes or editorial discussions, but with the urgency and honesty of our sharing, and a refreshing trust in each other's vision. We never had to set up extended rules of content. *Tangling with the Epic* was guided by our trust that something one of us offered, would have buried inside it a viable impetus for the other's "response". We did not set out a rule that said we would address each other directly in the work, it simply happened, and this way of not being literal about the use of the second person has been critical for us. The Spenserian stanza offered a quality of ritual and meditation that comes with the best of formal poetry. But finding a sincere music in this received form is what I believe to be the true accomplishment of this work.

The fact is that as you read these poems, you will encounter two men who begin as virtual strangers, men whose knowledge of each other has been limited to what we knew in biographies and in books, begin to learn each other through poetry, and in the process, to learn themselves. John and I have had access to each other's lives through poetry for four and a half years, and there is something exhilarating and comforting in knowing that this is a fair way of making fine poetry and friendship. In so many ways, we are pushed even more closely to what I believe is as true a voice as is trustworthy in poetry. We have, without stating it, held ourselves to a standard of political, ethical, aesthetic and imaginative integrity and honesty – we have agreed to write with the same fullness that we encounter our worlds. This intimacy is liberating and affirming, and fills me with gratitude.

KWAME RECOMMENDS

I've been in search of familiar beauty and reminders of feeling and delight: Martha Collins' *Because What Else Could I Do* (Pittsburgh University Press); John Kinsella's *Peripheral Light* (W.W. Norton); Derek Walcott's *The Fortunate Traveller* (Farrar Strauss and Giroux); *Gospels of Matthew, Mark, Luke and John*; Dionne Brand's *The Blue Clerk* (Duke University Press); Forest Gander's *Be With* (New Directions); Federico Garcia Lorca's *Poet in Spain,* a new translation by Sarah Arvio (Knopf); the democracy of the Academy of American Poets' online newsletter Poem-A-Day with its overwhelming ordinariness sparked by moments of genuine illumination; Romeo Oriogun's *Sacrament of Bodies* (University of Nebraska Press); Gbenga Adeoba's *Exodus* (University of Nebraska Press) and Ladan Osman's *Exiles of Eden* (Coffee House Press).

TANGLING WITH THE EPIC

44.

In the end we build edifices of truth
and lies, and happiness is made of what
we keep exposed and what we, unmoved
by guilt, keep hidden beneath sheltering hats.
I am made of nervous stock; thoughts like rats
dart through my mind, and words are prefects
who marshal them, keep them in line like brats
who will torment with their taunting whispers.
I can't know happiness without such painful muster.

KD

45.

With Federation driven by the White
Australia desire, I read we must see
the argument in and of its "times" – this blight
in the records of "history" – to free
thoughts of land-clearers in the colonies
and Alfred Deakin's "united race", "cast
of character", and that bold "unity
of Australia" bullshit? Residues? Vast
proof of how far we've come? And still in "race" *they* trust?

JK

Image: Sophie Davidson

DENISE RILEY

Denise Riley lives in London. She has written *War in the Nursery: Theories of the Child and Mother* (1983), *'Am I That Name?' Feminism and the Category of 'Women' in History* (1988), *The Words of Selves: Identification, Solidarity, Irony* (2000), *The Force of Language* with Jean-Jacques Lecercle (2004), *Impersonal Passion: Language as Affect* (2005) and *Time Lived, Without Its Flow* (2012). Her poetry collections include *Marxism for Infants* (1977), *Dry Air* (1985), *Mop Mop Georgette* (1993), *Penguin Modern Poets Volume 10*, with Douglas Oliver and Iain Sinclair (1996); *Selected Poems* (2000); *Say Something Back* (2016) and *Penguin Modern Poets Volume 6*, with Maggie Nelson and Claudia Rankine (2017).

SELECTED POEMS

PICADOR | £14.99 | PBS PRICE £11.25

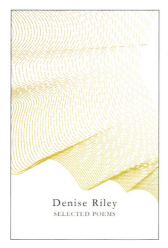

Denise Riley's latest *Selected Poems* brings together work from her 1977 Reality Street debut *Marxism for Infants* to her most recent book, *Say Something Back,* published by Picador in 2016. Although Reality Street, now defunct, brought out a *Selected* in 2000, this latest volume offers a wider range of Riley's back catalogue and keeps in circulation sections of books that are now rare or out of print, like the brilliant *Mop Mop Georgette.* As with any selection, though perhaps especially for Riley's work, decades of development divulge recurrent themes and ideas and, necessarily, make stylistic shifts visible against a changing poetic landscape from the 1970s to the present. The poems here form a conversation with Riley's work as a theorist who writes about women and feminism as well as poetic language. Riley is concerned with the social conditions of women, mothers especially, in her earlier works, but asks more broadly what classifies a woman's speech, what is "speech as a sexed thing"? Her poem 'Dark Looks' brings some of Riley's central concerns together with a characteristic wryness.

> Who anyone is or I am is nothing to the work. The writer
> properly should be the last person that the reader or the listener
> need think about
> yet the poet with her signature stands up trembling, grateful,
> mortally embarrassed
> and especially embarrassing to herself, patting her hair and
> twittering 'If, if only
> I need not have a physical appearance! To be sheer air, and
> mousseline!'

Finally this female writer deploys a heavily ironic plea – to be heard by the reader, knowing that this is what is expected of her but must be resisted (this 'I' who wishes to be sauce mousseline). Similarly in 'A note on sex and the 'reclaiming of language'' the woman returns to a simulacrum of home, a colonized land where she is now fetishized:

> The 'Savage' is flying back home from the New Country
> in native-style dress with a baggage of sensibility
> to gaze on the ancestral plains with the myths thought up
> and dreamed in her kitchens as guides

With this new edition Riley's interrogations will rightly provoke a new and wider audience for whom the terms of these debates have shifted, too.

24

SANDEEP PARMAR

DENISE RILEY

This selection covers almost five decades, from about 1976 to 2016. It includes work from my earlier *Selected Poems,* published in 2000 by the small press Reality Street, and the collection *Say Something Back* (Picador, 2016). *Say Something Back* is often described as "a book about bereavement", but only a third of it is concerned with death-related loss; the rest is about experiences of willed abandonment, or more often are cheerful notes of things seen. Although the writing does reflect on making your way in the light of familiar kinds of private loss, it tries to do so in a tone which isn't either melancholic or strongly autobiographical, but is open and undefended. My writing's preoccupations, including "song", seem to me to have stayed pretty much the same for ever. This poem 'Under the answering sky' is perhaps representative:

> I can manage being alone,
> can pace out convivial hope
> across my managing ground.
> Someone might call, later.
>
> What do the dead make of us
> that we'd flay ourselves trying
> to hear them though they may
> sigh at such close loneliness.
>
> I would catch, not my echo,
> but their guarantee that this
> bright flat blue is a mouth
> of the world speaking back.
>
> There is no depth to that blue.
> It won't 'bring the principle
> of darkness with it', but hums
> in repose, as radiant static.

Some of the other recent poems think aloud about rhyme's own relation to temporality, and how this links to that feeling of "time stopped" that you might inhabit after someone's unexpected death; this question recurs in my short prose essay, *Time Lived, Without Its Flow* (Picador, 2019). A collection of completely new work will, I hope, soon follow, but as yet it's only half-finished.

DENISE RECOMMENDS

As well as reading much new work originally written in English, I've also been re-reading Aimé Cesaire's *Return to My Native Land* (Bloodaxe), René Char's *Stone Lyre* (Tupelo Press), Gunter Eich's *Angina Days* (Facing Pages) and, with my gratitude to their translators, Kim Hyesoon's *Autobiography of Death* (New Directions), Krystyna Miłobędzka's *Nothing More* (Arc), Eugenio Montejo's *The Trees* (Salt), and Adélia Prado's *The Alphabet in the Park* (Weslyan University).

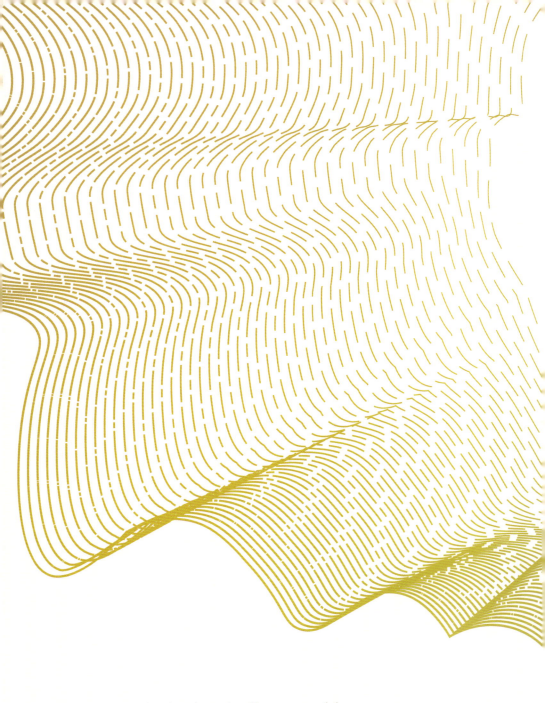

I dive into the broken brilliant world

THE AMBITION TO NOT BE PARTICULAR SPEAKS

'I cannot tell what gives each voice its tune –
some furious tenderness of buried words
or interference from the streets
and their hazardous crying –

but if for me some words must be exhumed
out of their sunken heat they must be cooled
to the grace of being common –

so to achieve my great colourlessness
I dive into the broken brilliant world
and float in it unindividuated, whitely'

Image: Anna Terék

ZOË SKOULDING

Zoë Skoulding is a poet, critic and translator who has lived in north Wales since 1991. Her collections of poetry include *The Mirror Trade* (Seren, 2004); *Remains of a Future City* (Seren, 2008), longlisted for Wales Book of the Year; *The Museum of Disappearing Sounds* (Seren, 2013), shortlisted for the Ted Hughes Award for New Work in Poetry; and *Teint: For the Bièvre* (Hafan Books, 2016). She is a Reader in the School of Languages, Literatures and Linguistics at Bangor University. In 2018 she was a recipient of the Cholmondeley Award from the Society of Authors for her contribution to poetry.

RECOMMENDATION

FOOTNOTES TO WATER

SEREN | £9.99 | PBS PRICE £7.50

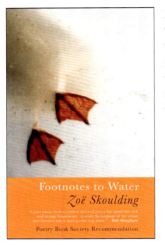

Zoë Skoulding dissents from the standard water-effects, that language of airbrushed flux we've heard before, and which reassuringly and ideologically separates the natural from the urban world. In her poetry, each line surprises, it doesn't soothe; her diction is conceptual and punning as well as mercurially sensuous:

> in its solitude the beach
> is a dead end not the way
> out or was it ever land-
> locked coffers sink and the slate
> glitters like all that isn't

This run-on style has a breathlessness to it; a historical connectedness hell-bent on excavation. In 'Gull Song':

> we come with eyes as cold as spreadsheets there is no warmth
> in our endless whiteness just the grey shadow of possession
> ...
> the too much of the takeaway the too many kebabs and chips
> we dance with your too many leftovers we are leftovers too
> with prehistoric feathers...

This is ecological and political stuff:

> You can see where the rock was cut away to build
> the shops, the upper slopes covered in wire to stop
> falling stones or branches. If one day it will be
> difficult to read in this landscape the difference
> between the effects of the movement of ice or
> water and those of the flow of capital, they are, at
> this moment, not to be confused...

'Confuse' derives, itself, from liquids running or mingling together: we use water to think with. "Water sleeps in every mirror. It / pulses under our feet, beneath car tyres, beneath sheds" – shaping, with our metaphors, our view of the world. Subjects recirculate (the river Adda, in particular); and while this book targets larger economies, it also considers the individual person:

> where I ran to you I
> ran as tainted water.

VIDYAN RAVINTHIRAN

ZOË SKOULDING

In this collection I'm interested in the line of a walk, and how that relates to the shape in which a poem emerges. The line I'm following might be a river, present or absent, or the looping tracks of sheep in a mountain landscape, but equally it might come from other texts or conversations along the way. Two sections of the book were written in parallel with different artists, Ben Stammers and Miranda Whall, and while the poems don't respond descriptively to their work, I've been in dialogue with ideas about site, performance and process from art practice. For this reason I've been drawn to the sequence, to poems that keep putting one foot in front of the other, rather than being a single event. I want the poem to open outwards, to the other lives and voices that intersect with its route. What kinds of attention are needed to make this possible? What have we already forgotten, even though we know it's still there?

Georges Perec's detailed notation of everyday phenomena has made me look again and look more closely at what might seem to be nothing happening, while Walter Benjamin's collection of fragmentary citation in *The Arcades Project* shows how language can be the site of the past erupting into the present. I think of the poem as this kind of terrain, one that is further contoured by the presence of more than one language.

Rivers, weather and birds move across borders. Humans aren't alone in their attachments to place but, as the hefting of sheep reveals, such attachments are learned rather than innate. Writing these poems has been a way of thinking about how belonging might be re-learned and extended, whether in the context of Wales and Europe or the non-human lives that are entangled with our own.

ZOË RECOMMENDS

Emily Critchley, *Arrangements* (Shearsman Books); Ian Davidson, *On the Way to Work* (Shearsman Books); Jeff Hilson, *Latanoprost Variations* (Boiler House Press); Kim Hyesoon, translated by Don Mee Choi, *Autobiography of Death* (New Directions); Bhanu Kapil, *Ban en Banlieu* (Nightboat); Shannon Maguire, editor, *Planetary Noise: Selected Poetry of Erín Moure* (Wesleyan University Press); Rod Mengham, *2019 the vase in pieces* (Oystercatcher); Nat Raha, *of sirens, body & faultlines* (Boiler House Press); Víctor Rodríguez Núñez, translated by Kate Hedeen, *Tasks* (Co-Im-Press).

RECOMMENDATION

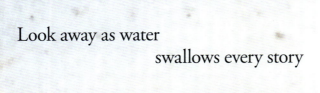

Look away as water
swallows every story

Image: Ben Stammers

TEINT

I

Not a river but its
                    shadow harmonics hidden
level in the glass note
                    glissando between a
movement and a sound
                    half in the performance
where I ran to you I
                    ran as tainted water

while tarmac shines in rain
                    the channels you don't touch
well up on tomorrow's
                    tongue to flower there don't
leave or was it this way
                    that now I'll run from you

CHARLOTTE MEW

Charlotte Mew (1869–1928) was an English short-story writer and poet. Born in Bloomsbury into a middle-class Victorian family, her work was published and admired both in the UK and in America. The first and only book to appear in her lifetime, *The Farmer's Bride*, came out in 1916 when she was in her mid-forties. On the strength of it, Mew was awarded a Civil List pension, with recommendations from three of her most ardent admirers: Poet Laureate John Masefield, Walter de la Mare and Thomas Hardy.

Julia Copus has published four poetry collections, including *The World's Two Smallest Humans* (2012), shortlisted for the T.S. Eliot Prize and the Costa Poetry Award, and *Girlhood* (2019). She has won First Prize in the National Poetry Competition and the Forward Prize for Best Single Poem. She works as a freelance podcast producer and, in 2018, was made a Fellow of the Royal Society of Literature.

CHARLOTTE MEW, ED. JULIA COPUS

FABER | £14.99 | PBS PRICE £11.25

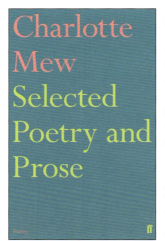

A neglected genius, Charlotte Mew did not publish before 1901, and died in 1928, but many of her masterpieces were probably written between the springs of 1913 and 1914. She's a modern poet: lucidly profound, brisk, though never brusque, in utterance; concerned with emotional scissions that align with hierarchies – the changing relation, for example, between men and women – but which also express psychological quirks.

'The Farmer's Bride' is one of the great poems of the twentieth-century. He – the farmer – is baffled: "when us was wed she turned afraid / Of love and me and all things human; / Like the shut of a winter's day / Her smile went out, and 'twasn't a woman". The rhyme of "human" and "woman" disturbs, as in the work of Stevie Smith: he thinks her animal. "We caught her, fetched her home at last, / And turned the key upon her, fast":

> She does the work about the house
> As well as most, but like a mouse:
> > Happy enough to chat and play
> > With birds and rabbits and such as they,
> > So long as men-folk keep away.
> 'Not near, not near!' her eyes beseech
> When one of us comes within reach.
> > The women say that beasts in stall
> > Look round like children at her call.
> > *I've* hardly heard her speak at all.

"When one of us comes within reach": the change of rhythm – an iamb, then two anapests – marvellously captures a spoken tone, keeping the couplet limber; and with the petulant last line we sense the entitlement of the speaker, his nursed grievance. His silent bride steals his power, and Mew is the master of such reversals:

> Give me the key that locks your tired eyes,
> > And I will lend you this one from my pack,
> Brighter than coloured beads and painted books that make
> > men wise:
> Take it. No, give it back!

VIDYAN RAVINTHIRAN

THE CALL

From our low seat beside the fire
　　Where we have dozed and dreamed and watched the glow
　Or raked the ashes, stopping so
We scarcely saw the sun or rain
　　Above, or looked much higher
Than this same quiet red or burned-out fire.
　　　　To-night we heard a call,
　　　A rattle on the window-pane,
　　　A voice on the sharp air,
And felt a breath stirring our hair,
　　A flame within us: Something swift and tall
　Swept in and out and that was all.
Was it a bright or a dark angel? Who can know?
　It left no mark upon the snow,
　　　But suddenly it snapped the chain
　　　Unbarred, flung wide the door
　　　Which will not shut again;
And so we cannot sit here any more.
　　　We must arise and go:
　　The world is cold without
　　And dark and hedged about
　　With mystery and enmity and doubt,
　　　　But we must go
　　Though yet we do not know
Who called, or what marks we shall leave upon the snow.

ESTHER DISCHEREIT

Esther Dischereit was born in 1952 in Germany and lives in Berlin. A poet, novelist, essayist, stage and radio dramatist, her works include *When My Golem Opened the Door*, *Hoarfrosted Mouth and Other News*, *There's a Slice of Bread in the Toaster* and *Lessons in Being Jewish*. Esther Dischereit was a fellow at the Moses Mendelssohn Centre for European and Jewish Studies and the Deutsches Haus New York and has lectured widely in the United States and Canada. In 2009 Esther Dischereit received the Erich-Fried-Prize. A symposium about her work was held at the University of Wales, Swansea, in 2003.

SOMETIMES A SINGLE LEAF
ESTHER DISCHEREIT, TRANSLATED BY IAIN GALBRAITH
ARC   PUBLICATIONS | £9.99 | PBS   PRICE   £7.50

In his introduction, her translator, Iain Galbraith, refers to a single line poem in which the speaker departs, leaving behind certain splinters. These splinters, he argues appear in poems that are "simple enough at first glance, but leave a puzzling or troubling trace on the reading consciousness". Splinters are tiny pieces of wreckage that can cause hurt. One may come across a splinter without knowing quite where it came from. In the case of consciousness it may be a product of something within the self or something outside that has entered the self. In terms of poetry, the damage implies some complex of the two. One does not read the poem in order to identify the condition of the poet but because such splintering reflects an experience we can, at least, partly, identify.

Dischereit, a German poet of Jewish background, has talked about "a Cubist gaze", of seeing something severally at the same time. The splinters might be products of her familial and tribal history. Whatever has splintered, the splinters are in us, or in the poet's case, in the poetry it produces. They may appear in sudden shifts of focus or in the apprehension of ambiguities. "One day we crept up the staircase / into my frenzied heart", she writes, in a sequence titled 'Moon and Blue'. And, later, in the same poem, "My mouth / bleeds out / on / soft words". "I fall upon the thorns of life, I bleed" wrote Shelley in 'Ode to the West Wind', a line at the very core of Romantic poetry. It can sound self-pitying, a public display of vulnerability. But that is not the core of Dischereit's poetry. The vulnerability is in the world and the self is in the world.

> I saw in an ice-white
> garden the winter light
> had coloured
> the yellow rose and its stalk...

Galbraith talks of Sachs, Celan, Kolmar, Fried and Lasker-Schüler. We are in that order of experience and articulation. It is history at work.

SOMETIMES A SINGLE LEAF

Sometimes a single leaf
sails to the ground, caught
by an air plume and released
I dance after the leaf
and cannot remember the steps
I falter, arms flailing
the leaf will not fly again
as it did this once
no leaf will fly like this one.
As I recently told you

Manchmal segelt ein einzelnes Blatt
zu Boden von Luftschlieren gefangen
und wieder freigegeben
ich tanze dem Blatt hinterher
und kann mir die Schritte nicht merken
ich strauchele, rudere mit den Armen
das Blatt wird nicht wieder fliegen
wie dies eine Mal
kein Blatt wird fliegen wie dies eine.
Hab ich dir neulich gesagt.

AMY ACRE

Amy Acre is a poet and performer from London, and the editor of Bad Betty Press. Her poem, 'every girl knows' won the 2019 Verve Poetry Prize. Her first pamphlet, *Where We're Going, We Don't Need Roads* (flipped eye) was a Poetry Book Society Pamphlet Choice and a Poetry School Book of 2015. She has performed at Southbank and the Houses of Parliament, on BBC Radio, and co-edited anthologies *The Dizziness of Freedom* and *Alter Egos* (Bad Betty Press) and the *Anti-Hate Anthology* (Spoken Word London).

AND THEY ARE COVERED IN GOLD LIGHT

BAD   BETTY   PRESS | £6.00

Amy Acre's latest pamphlet, *And They Are Covered in Gold Light*, is a blistering exploration of the facades and personas we adopt to function and survive in a dysfunctional world. The opening poem 'Your Concerns are Very Important to Us' is punctuated with affectionate terms ("bae", "sweetheart") that build a sense of intimacy and warmth, alleviating the darkness that permeates the collection. Throughout, Acre's voice shines with modernity and humour, and it's this light touch that allows her to explore serious themes and create detailed portraits of complex women. For example, Mary in the wonderfully titled, 'Mary's Holding Jesus, Not Like a God but Like a Baby, Like I Would Hold My Baby':

> when he blessed her
> she wanted to spit in his face
> tell him boy
> i'm the one who wiped away your shit

In the award-winning prose poem 'every girl knows', Acre lays bare the excitement and dangers of young womanhood. Her precise descriptions creating a vivid portrayal of vulnerable but street savvy teens navigating their way through a world where they are sexualised and commodified. Acre delights in playing with visceral imagery and the fierce women in 'The Happy Princesses' reminded me of Vicki Feaver's poem 'Judith', subverting the idea of "princesses" as passive and delicate.

> chiomara carried
> her rapist's head
> in the dust of her dress
> let it rest in her lap

The final poem sequence 'When Your Name is a Knife' is an essential, unflinching look at the sinister narratives playing out on the edges of society where people are searching for something or someone to fill the void. It is suspenseful and has a driving energy that is a fitting end to a collection, which although full of rage, is also filled with hope and defiance.

> no
> Her body is fearless
> reclaiming paradigms
> she stares you out

44   A.B. JACKSON & DEGNA STONE

YOUR CONCERNS ARE VERY IMPORTANT TO US

on the way to the kitchen i realise i am no longer in my body.
all bodies contain some amount of negative space.
it's ambiguous whether this is you or near you.
on this occasion i pour into the absence, dragging a dead bird,
and the absence receives me like a hostile border force officer.
months later love skirts around the entrance, brandishing an email
confirmation which must be exchanged for a ticket,
skinny jeans gone grey across the knees and bae, i get it.
we are both jealous gods. i too have buckled at empty temples
wondering in which room i would find the 'like a prayer' video.
i remember the covenant, pyrotechnics, everything that falls if you let it
but sweetheart, gravity exists whether or not you believe.
sweetheart, why don't you reach inside yourself to push
your fallen organs back in and tell me if you feel holy.

MIMI KHALVATI

Mimi Khalvati was born in Tehran, Iran, and has lived most of her life in London. She has published eight collections with Carcanet Press, including *The Meanest Flower*, shortlisted for the T.S. Eliot Prize 2007; *Child: New and Selected Poems 1991-2011*, a Poetry Book Society Special Commendation; and *The Weather Wheel*, a Poetry Book Scoiety Recommendation and a Book of the Year in *The Independent*. Her pamphlet *Earthshine* (Smith/Doorstop Books, 2013) was a Poetry Book Society Pamphlet Choice and her *Very Selected Poems* was published by Smith/ Doorstop in 2017. She won a Cholmondeley Award from the Society of Authors, a major Arts Council Writer's Award, and is the founder of the Poetry School, a Fellow of the Royal Society of Literature and of The English Society.

AFTERWARDNESS

CARCANET | £9.99 | PBS PRICE £7.50

In Mimi Khalvati's latest collection, *Afterwardness*, the poet can be seen to focus on both the public and the private world. Language often textured with a sense of distance or perspective still manages to connect with its subjects. In neat sequences of poems ranging from the anecdotal to the philosophical and existential, Khalvati conjures a dazzling array of images in order to help revivify the commonplace, attributing additional significance to her extended metaphysical family – and quotidian matters are never too far off. In the poem 'Jolanta', "Between times, plants get watered, piles of paper shrink or grow and a vase might spring sweetpeas." Throughout the book there is a noticeable reckoning with the inevitable – of age, time, abandonment, loneliness and resilience.

Cafes

Envy them, the lonely, there by the glass,
there in the corner, staring into space
for as long as it takes the world to pass,
close up, far off, sprinkled like stars in cafés.

Khalvati's poems present as two sets of quatrains above two tercets, giving the impression of moments compact and belonging, while also establishing control in the face of what is being orbited. "A farawayness surfaces like a shoal" we're told in the poem 'Outpatients' with its stark, mesmeric imagery drawing on cardiology, a lone fisherman and Boris Johnson's great grandfather Ali Kemal. What is particularly striking throughout the collection is how the poems are able to move through time in relation to one's age, life or nationality. Certain pieces focus on the speaker's childhood, on family and parents, while others seem to possess an oracular quality, 'The Artist as a Child' tells us "Neither love nor fear can be drawn to scale." In 'The Brag' the poem does a stellar job in fusing all the book's complex and overlapping ideas into a singular piece:

Some call me lady, auntie, mammie – ask me
how I'm doing, endorse me with endearments,
watch my footing for me, rescue my bag.

| SELECTOR'S COMMENT | ANTHONY ANAXAGOROU

MIMI KHALVATI

Losing my mother tongue at a young age, and with it the memories encoded in that language, has meant that I remember little of my first six years in Iran before being sent to boarding school on the Isle of Wight. And growing up without the habit of autobiographical memory, without family to act as witness, to fill in family background, has also left me without a clear sense of my own life story. But I do have a remembered sensation of being on the plane that brought me to England and *Afterwardness* takes this first flight as its starting point.

I have always lived with a sense of a void at the centre of my life – not only a space of absence and loss, but a vast sky of longing, love, desire. Poems have drifted to me out of this dreamspace, randomly, out of the present moment or out of the past. And I have allowed them to go where they will, to discover how to give value to a life lived without the ballast of a clear story, especially at a time of mass migration and displacement when to tell our stories is so paramount.

For my themes, I have drawn gratefully on *Third Culture Kids* by David C. Pollock, Ruth E. Van Reken and Michael V. Pollock. Though oblique, they have formed a silent substrate out of which a first line might float up. There are fifty-six hybrid sonnets here, a series which I hope some readers will read straight through. I have respected the proportions of the Italian sonnet throughout (with an English rhyme scheme in the octet), the Petrarchan sonnet feeling more mercurial to me, more likely to tackle the question: How do you change something without changing it? – in art, if not in life.

MIMI RECOMMENDS

In loving memory, I recommend Carole Satyamurti's landmark verse translation, *Mahabharata* (W.W. Norton); also Marilyn Hacker, *Blazons* (Carcanet); Faisal Mohyuddin, *The Displaced Children of Displaced Children* (Eyewear); Maitreyabandhu, *After Cézanne* (Bloodaxe); Lucy Hamilton, *Of Heads & Hearts* (Shearsman); Seni Seneviratne, *Unknown Soldier* (Peepal Tree); Maria Jastrzębska, *The True Story of Cowboy Hat and Ingénue* (Cinnamon Press); Mona Arshi, *Dear Big Gods* (Pavilion); Tracy K. Smith, *Eternity* (Penguin) and Vidyan Ravinthiran, *The Million-petalled Flower of Being Here* (Bloodaxe).

GUEST REVIEWER: JADE CUTTLE

FRANK ORMSBY: THE RAIN BARREL

In Frank Ormsby's seventh collection of poems, a majestic charm is cast across the Irish landscape and the small farms among which he grew up, elevating the fowl on the lake and the flooded hollows to delightful heights of enchantment. Ormsby's deeply intimate connection to his surroundings is both sensual and self-aware, openly suspicious of the delicate language of tenderness, whilst poignantly drawing on the continuing violence and conflict of Northern Ireland after The Troubles.

BLOODAXE BOOKS | £12.00 | PBS PRICE £9.00

HEATHER CHRISTLE: THE TREES, THE TREES

In this wistfully lyrical collection, Christle tends to the fragments of selfhood with an ethereal, dreamlike sensibility. Speaking out with stream-of-conscious urgency, the body is exposed as half-human, half-other and held together by holes. As though gazing up through a luscious canopy of green, each poem becomes a vivid spectacle of play and patchwork, as the form itself is flawlessly consistent in mirroring the mesmeric tapestry of trees.

CORSAIR BOOKS | £10.99 | PBS PRICE £8.25

THE RESULT IS WHAT YOU SEE TODAY
POEMS ABOUT RUNNING

A tour-de-force celebration of tracks and trails, edited by Ben Wilkinson, Kim Moore and Paul Deaton, this exhilarating anthology doesn't just focus on distance, die-hard sprints and dog walking. From wood-legged cross-countriers to a Club Run led by Dante and fellow sinners, this collection gives voice to a wide range of legends and losers alike. Enduring endless laps and lashing rain, it provides an uplifting insight into the power of endurance and the prize of euphoria.

SMITH | DOORSTOP | £10.00 | PBS PRICE   £7.50

WINTER BOOK REVIEWS

DAN BURT: SALVAGE AT TWILIGHT

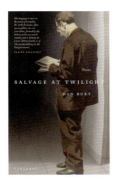

This moving collection marks the poet's own journey from a harsh upbringing in Philadephia's slums ("Dad taught me to steal when I turned twelve") to Cambridge and Yale Law School. Interspersing poetry with prose memoir, Burt reveals how life shapes art. His terse verse is often formed by "rage, and cold control", but beneath the fighting talk a deeper humanity shines through. No more so than in the final sequence 'Salvages', where lost family and friends are memorialised in vivid vignettes.

CARCANET PRESS | £9.99 | PBS PRICE £7.50

VICKY FEAVER: I WANT! I WANT!

Inspired by Blake's illustration of a child climbing a ladder to the moon, *I Want! I Want!* vividly evokes the poet's childhood growing up after the war. Through fairytale figures – a Snow Queen and a Mermaid – Feaver charts her own coming-of-age as a female poet: "a woman buried under ice / with words burning inside". Blake's ladder motif recurs throughout, signalling new sequences. These are her own Blakean songs of innocence and experience, which bravely face the past, present and future.

CAPE | £10.00 | PBS PRICE £7.50

PAUL FARLEY: THE MIZZY

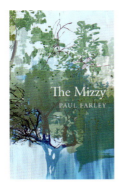

This collection begins with 'Starling', a self-criticism of the poet's regionalism: "[I] witter on about my hole in the wall, // the place where I'm from, to any bird that would listen." Farley immediately responds to this challenge, to sweep across a range of subjects with imaginative panache. He still has certain roots, like a playpark ship which "couldn't set sail from this dry dock", and familiar preoccupations with liminality run throughout. This is hardly a failing; it's a joy to read a master at work, with deft use of extended metaphor, imagery and rhythm.

PICADOR | £14.99 HB | PBS PRICE £11.25

WINTER BOOK REVIEWS

Functioning like a cosmic map from the level of sub-atomic particles to vast celestial bodies, *Edge* succeeds at wedding the arts with science to create a mesmerising and transportive collection. Porteous makes precise and artful use of scientific terminology to complement her sparse and tightly constructed verse. The full effect is to bring the reader to a state of communion; to instil a sense of beauty and belonging to the world of particles, fields, waves, and the behaviour of massive gravitational bodies.

BLOODAXE BOOKS | £12.00 | PBS PRICE £9.00

LEGNA RODRÍGUEZ IGLESIAS: A LITTLE BODY ARE MANY PARTS
TRANSLATED BY ABIGAIL PARRY & SERAFINA VICK

This daring dual language collection by an award-winning Cuban poet explores the rebellious power and vulnerability of words, "I've been writing, grandfather / And that is my revolution". Full of surreal, playful and perplexing imagery, Iglesias skewers society and the poetic mind: "The chickens of disquiet, pecking". *A little body are many parts* challenges taboos to celebrate the female body, in all its grotesque glory, with a fierce determination to be "a free human being".

BLOODAXE | £12.00 | PBS PRICE £9.00

A feeling of crisis pervades this collection from the author of previous PBS Pamphlet Choice, *Complicity*. Amid personal, social, political and environmental collapse, Sastry brings a signature voice, eloquent and direct, brimming with deep ironies and anguishes. "Do not listen to the sea," he writes, "It hides plastics // and weapons of mass destruction." The allure and the peril of denial, the modern state of feeling utterly lost, of being unable to find answers, are significant concerns in this troubling and vital work.

NINE ARCHES PRESS | £9.95 | PBS PRICE £7.47

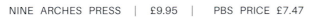

| WINTER READING

Gathering a range of collaborative place projects between the poet Harriet Tarlo and the artist Judith Tucker, these formally fascinating poems follow the curve of a valley or the flow of a "stream song" with crystalline precision. Tarlo traces changing landscapes from the "snow-curved / space" of Winter to "slow-grown Spring", capturing wider ecological issues and the shifting relationship of people and place. This is a vital, urgent and immersive read for our age of climate emergency.

SHEARSMAN | £14.95 | PBS PRICE £11.22

NATALIE SCOTT: RARE BIRDS - VOICES OF HOLLOWAY PRISON

In a fascinating sequence of dramatic monologues, Scott inhabits the voices of inmates from a hundred years of Holloway Prison, which became a women's prison in 1902. Contained here are imaginings of the inner thoughts of historical figures like Sylvia Pankhurst and Emily Wilding Davidson, as well as voices forgotten to time. Found poems and rich accompanying notes further bring to life the prison's dark and intriguing history.

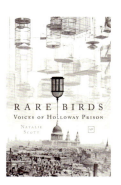

VALLEY PRESS | £12.00 | PBS PRICE £9.00

TAMAR YOSELOFF: THE BLACK PLACE

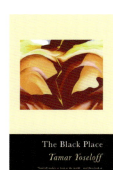

Art, including the titular painting by Georgia O'Keeffe, provides one of many points of anchorage on Yoseloff's meditative journey through bleak urban hinterlands and dread-imbued pastoral landscapes. Two notable points of reference in this collection are the poet's cancer diagnosis and the Grenfell tower disaster, occurring concurrently and provoking a measured and elegant response to the nature of grief and fear. Yoseloff's dextrous wordplay adds wings to an accomplished, moving collection.

SEREN | £9.99 | PBS PRICE £7.50

WINTER PAMPHLETS

RISHI DASTIDAR: THE BREAK OF A WAVE

This small, perfectly formed pamphlet contains ten artfully composed windows onto miniature worlds and brief moments in time. By degrees playful, wistful and mournful, Dastidar takes as his subject a variety of intimacies, of moments between lovers. A tantalising and evocative sequence accompanied by a striking photographic series.

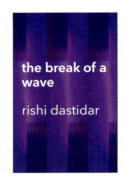

the break of a wave

rishi dastidar

OFFORD ROAD BOOKS | £4.00 |

ZAFFAR KUNIAL: SIX

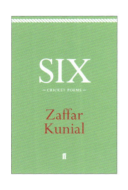

SIX

— CRICKET POEMS —

Zaffar Kunial

ff

Zaffar Kunial grew up near the Edgbaston cricket ground in Birmingham, so it seems highly fitting that he was recently appointed the official Poet in Residence at The Oval. In these six new cricket inspired poems, Kunial merges sport and nostalgia to narrate childhood, family history and identity. Through these charming cricket poems the reader finds "a world restored." This is an ideal stocking filler for fans of cricket and poetry alike.

FABER | £6.00 |

MICHAEL LONGLEY: A STREAM'S TATTLE

This delicate, contemplative pamphlet from multiple award-winning poet Michael Longley is the perfect short collection for a nature-lover. As well as being appreciated in their own right, natural spaces form a backdrop for memory, for musings upon the persistent rush of time, the ephemerality of physical existence. This is most heart-breakingly encapsulated by a poem dedicated to his daughter: "I am running out of rhymes, // O fifty-year old daughter, // And I am running out of time."

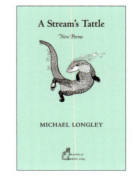

A Stream's Tattle

New Poems

MICHAEL LONGLEY

MARISCAT PRESS | £6.00 |

IAN McMILLAN: THAT'S NOT A FISHING BOAT, IT'S A GIRAFFE: RESPONSES TO AUSTERITY

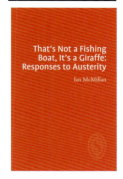

With hints of Spike Milligan and Monty Python, McMillan unleashes his own brand of absurdism against the equally absurd world of current affairs. More tragi-comic than comic, these poems cut to the quick of political cynicism, social deprivation, ignorance and xenophobia. A necessary yet entertaining response to our age of political anxiety.

SMITH | DOORSTOP | £6.00 |

REBECCA PERRY: BEACHES

This striking pamphlet by a former T.S. Eliot prize nominee is haunted by a sequence of surreal beaches and littoral edges: "I walked to the water / to wash / to relocate my voice". The spectre of the sea is both restorative and oddly unsettling. An unknown anxiety seeps through these shorelines –"people / orbit the griever"– and an ebb and flow of estrangement. Nothing is quite as it seems but it's well worth grappling with these shifting sands.

OFFORD ROAD | £5.00 |

CHRISTMAS SPIRIT: TEN POEMS TO WARM THE HEART

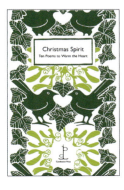

No one does Christmas quite as well as Candlestick Press! This year they present ten specially commissioned new poems to celebrate the joy of Christmas, from the inevitable untangling of fairy lights to wrapping presents and ancient seasonal traditions. This heart-warming anthology is guaranteed to rekindle your Christmas spirit with poems by Fleur Adcock, Seán Hewitt, Theophilus Kwek, Katrina Porteous and James Sheard. The perfect gift for poetry lovers this Christmas.

CANDLESTICK PRESS | £4.95 |

PAMPHLET REVIEWS

WINTER LISTINGS
NEW BOOKS

AUTHOR	TITLE	PUBLISHER	RRP
Juana Adcock	Split	Blue Diode Press	£10.00
Jane Aldous	Let Out the Djinn	Arachne Press	£8.99
Charlotte Ansell	Deluge	flipped eye publishing	£6.95
Tessa Berring	Bitten Hair	Blue Diode Press	£10.00
Ed. by Nisha Bhakoo	The Emma Press Anthology of Contemporary Gothic Verse	The Emma Press	£10.00
Jhilmil Breckenridge	Reclamation Song	Verve Poetry Press	£9.99
Eleanor Brown	White Ink Stains	Bloodaxe Books	£9.95
Sue Brown	Rhythm Chant	Verve Poetry Press	£9.99
Dan Burt	Salvage At Twilight	Carcanet Press	£12.99
James Byrne	The Caprices	Arc Publications	£10.99
Nora Chassler	Itheherome	Valley Press	£12.00
Heather Christle	The Trees The Trees	Corsair Books	£10.99
Ed. by Urszula Clark & Jonathan Davidson	Spake	Nine Arches Press	£10.99
Douglas Crase	The Revisionist and The Astropastorals	Carcanet Press	£12.99
Ralph Dartford	Recovery Songs	Valley Press	£9.99
Ed. by Rishi Dastidar	The Craft: A Guide to Making Poetry Happen in the 21st Century	Nine Arches Press	£14.99
Kwame Dawes & John Kinsella	Tangling with the Epic	Peepal Tree Press	£10.99
Nichola Deane	Cuckoo	V. Press	£10.99
Ed. by Paul Deaton, Kim Moore & Ben Wilkinson	The Result Is What You See Today: Poems about Running	Smith|Doorstop	£10.00
Ed. by Chiamaka Enyi-Amadi & Pat Boran	Writing Home	Dedalus Press	£12.95
Anthony Etherin	Stray Arts (And Other Inventions)	Penteract Press	£14.00
Paul Farley	The Mizzy	Picador	£14.99
Vicki Feaver	I Want! I Want!	Jonathan Cape	£10.00
Wesley Franz	Megaglorations	Maida Vale Publishing	£10.99
Chrissie Gittins	Sharp Hills	Indigo Dreams	£9.99
Charles G Lauder	The Aesthetics of Breath	V. Press	£10.99
Sue Hyon Bae	Truce Country	Eyewear Publishing	£10.99
Luke Jacobs	The Seed Vault	Eyewear Publishing	£10.99
Mimi Khalvati	Afterwardness	Carcanet Press	£9.99
Patrick Lodge	Remarkable Occurrences	Valley Press	£12.00
Jessica Mayhem	Longship	Eyewear Publishing	£10.99
Charlotte Mew	Selected Poetry and Prose	Faber & Faber	£14.99
John Montague	Selected Poems: 1961-2017	The Gallery Press	£12.50
Lucy Newlyn	Vital Stream	Carcanet Press	£12.99
Eiléan Ní Chuilleanáin	The Mother House	The Gallery Press	£10.50
Frank Ormsby	The Rain Barrel	Bloodaxe Books	£12.00
Katrina Porteous	Edge	Bloodaxe Books	£12.00
Denise Riley	Selected Poems	Picador	£14.99
Michael Rosen	Mr Mensh	Smokestack Books	£8.95
Tom Sastry	A Man's House Catches Fire	Nine Arches Press	£9.99
Natalie Scott	Rare Birds: Voices of Holloway Prison	Valley Press	£12.00
Zoë Skoulding	Footnotes to Water	Seren	£9.99
Kelley Swain	Darwin's Microscope	Valley Press	£12.00
Harriet Tarlo	Gathering Grounds	Shearsman Books	£14.95
Mariah Whelan	the love I do to you	Eyewear Publishing	£10.99
Robin Lindsay Wilson	Backstage in Paradise	Cinnamon Press	£9.99
Tamar Yoseloff	The Black Place	Seren	£9.99